Night-Night

Night-Night

Settle-Down Activities
for Easy Bedtimes

CYNTHIA MacGREGOR

Foreword by June Rifkin

CONARI PRESS
Berkeley, California

Conari Press books are distributed by Publishers Group West.

Cover and Interior Illustrations: Gary Phillips
Cover and Book Design: Claudia Smelser

Library of Congress Cataloging-in-Publication Data

MacGregor, Cynthia.
    Night-night : settle-down activities for easy bedtimes / Cynthia MacGregor.
        p.   cm.
    ISBN 1-57324-754-5
    1. Children—Sleep.   2. Child rearing.   I. Title.
    BF723.S45 M23 2001
    649'.4—dc21   2001001910

Printed in the United States of America on recycled paper.
01   02   03   DATA   10   9   8   7   6   5   4   3   2   1

For Laurel
Use it well . . . and enjoy!

Night-Night

Foreword

by June Rifkin, editor of *The Everything Mother Goose Book*

Let's face it—as grown-ups, we relish the idea of sleep. At the end of a long, hard day, there's nothing more satisfying than fluffing up our pillows and peacefully drifting off to dreamland, where we can forget about the cares and woes of the day and rest our weary minds. If only our young children felt the same way!

Children, especially toddlers through school aged, have boundless energy and are taking in the world around them every waking hour of their day. Sleep? Unless they suddenly succumb to exhaustion on the living room sofa or in the car seat on the ride home from Grandma's, they have no conscious desire to say "Good night." Kids have lots of valid reasons to *not* want to go to bed. They might be afraid of the dark or of being alone in their rooms . . . worried or excited about something that's happening the next day . . . or aware that something special is going on "after hours" and they want to stay up with Mom or Dad and not miss out on grown-up fun. Whatever the reason, how do we find new and interesting ways to help our kids relax and look forward to bedtime as much as we do?

In *Night-Night: Settle-Down Activities for Easy Bedtimes,* Cynthia MacGregor provides a myriad of delightful activities that will help children pleasantly ease into bedtime. From storytelling to silly songs and rhymes, soothing games, and innovative thinking exercises, these wonderful ideas will help kids relax, get them thinking creatively, and most important, create a special bond between parents and children.

The concepts and activities outlined in *Night-Night* were developed by MacGregor and other parents and used successfully to make bedtimes easier and more fun. Many of the games and activities are educational in nature, helping young children build skills with letters, spelling, numbers, and geography, and even inspire cognitive thinking. Other activities engage children in the creation of a story or game or song. For example, "And Now for the News . . ." allows children to "broadcast" their special news of the day from the comfort of their own beds, while "Good-Night,

Teddy" encourages children to put their favorite stuffed animals or dolls to bed before they settle down for the night.

In today's busy and often stressful world, weeknights, in particular, can leave us with limited quality time to share with our children. *Night-Night* not only offers creative solutions to the challenges of bedtime but also gives parents unique and enjoyable ways to foster closer relationships with their children. Bedtime becomes a delightful and special part of the day, where we can share special one-on-one time with our children.

Adults need downtime too, and *Night-Night* offers parents the opportunity for end-of-day relaxation that benefits them too. Let's hope the grownups don't fall asleep before their kids do!

Acknowledgments

I wish to thank for their help and ideas (in alphabetical order): Phyllis Johnson, Ron Wiggins, Tiff Wimberly, and Janice Wisdom.

Introduction: Bedtime Made Easy

Getting a child to bed—and to sleep—is a two-part chore . . . and neither part is easy. The first part is simply getting her into bed; the second part is keeping her there.

You can carry an infant to bed (although that doesn't always guarantee he'll go to sleep when you want him to), but once a child is of walking age and out of a crib, once you're no longer carrying him to his bed but telling him to go, getting him there can be a tribulation. And getting him to stay in bed till he falls asleep can be even more problematic. You know all the dodges by now: He wants water. She has to go to the bathroom. He needs you to check for monsters under his bed. If he's in school or day care, he may have a note from his teacher that he forgot to show you till now. Or she may simply wander back out to the living room, proclaiming loudly that she just isn't sleepy.

Kids resist bedtime for a variety of reasons, ranging from fear of bad dreams or monsters or darkness to worry that they'll miss something interesting or enjoyable while they're sleeping. And sometimes they really aren't tired or sleepy enough yet . . . or they're so wound up that they can't relax enough to go to sleep. We've all seen the child who insists she's not sleepy, insists some more, then suddenly falls asleep in the middle of the floor.

In getting your child successfully to sleep, you have two goals: The first is to make going to bed a pleasurable activity, so your child will be more willing; the second is to get your child relaxed enough that she can fall asleep with a minimum of difficulty.

That's what this book will help you with.

If you're tired of bedtime battles with your three- to ten-year-old, this book is for you. The bedtime activities suggested here all make bedtime a pleasure and help kids relax once they're snuggled in bed.

It's no secret that a child who's been racing around the house for the last ten minutes isn't going to turn on a dime, stop short, and go docilely off to bed when you suddenly announce, "It's bedtime. Go to sleep." You can try to call a sudden halt to her wild activity, kiss her goodnight, and tell her to get in her pajamas and get ready to be tucked in. You can even take her to her room and help her get ready. But not only is it a problem to get a wound-up child in bed; when she does get under the covers you likely haven't seen the last of her for the night.

He'll be back out in just a few minutes—or he'll be sitting up in bed calling for you. He may say he wants a glass of water or something to eat; he may have some other request. The real problem is that his engine is still running at high speed. How can he relax and go to sleep when he's still so revved up?

Even kids who've been playing a quiet game or watching TV for the last half-hour aren't always able to settle down and go right off to sleep. The body may be reasonably relaxed, but the mind may not be. Or his mind may kick into high gear when he lies down and lets his thoughts begin to wander. Whether it's a three-year-old worried about monsters under the bed, a five-year-old afraid of the howling wind, a six-year-old concerned about what the school bully will do tomorrow, or an eight-year-old dreading a spelling test, a child whose mind is filled with worries and fears is a child who isn't going to drift off to sleep quickly.

You probably limit your child's consumption of soda and other sugary treats for a reasonable period of time before bed. You know not to chase your child around the house in a high-spirited game or engage him in a pillow fight or any other activity that will rev him up just before bedtime. You know that if you want to get him settled into bed with any chance of success, what he does shortly beforehand is important. But you also know that, no matter how hard you try, there are some nights—perhaps in your home it's *every* night—when he either resists going to bed or resists staying there.

When I put out the call for "bedtime activities other than reading a book" to parents I know—and to friends of friends of friends (writers of this sort of book tend to have wide-reaching circles!)—I got remarkably few helpful answers. I did get a lot of, "When that book is published, I want it!" And I got far too much of, "In our house, the bedtime activity is screaming. I say that it's bedtime, and the kids say that they're not sleepy, and the result is inevitably a fight."

In the cases where the question was asked face to face (rather than by phone or e-mail), I got a lot of surprised looks, usually accompanied by some variation of, "You mean . . . doing something other than telling her a story when I put her to bed?" Any number of these parents readily admitted that their kids were no longer enchanted with the prospect of hearing a story every night, yet the parents had never thought to vary the routine.

Bedtime stories are the most traditional pre-sleep activity . . . and they're a good one. And apparently, for many people, it's hard to buck tradition, even when the advantage of doing so would seem obvious. The promise of a bedtime story has lured kids to bed for centuries, and focusing on Cinderella or Robin Hood gives kids something to occupy their minds with till sleep comes to claim them . . . which can happen more easily when they're relaxed and thinking of something nice.

There are several other reasons for the continuing popularity of bedtime stories as a nighttime ritual. The activity accomplishes a number of good things at one time:

- It fosters a closer bond between the two of you.

- It helps instill a love of stories that one hopes will translate into a love of reading as the child gets older.

- And last, but not least, the nighttime story provides a good settling-down ritual for the child. As he concentrates on the story, his body can relax in bed, and his mind can relax too. Focused on the book you're reading to her, she isn't worried about what's going to happen the next day in school or whether the closet monster is lying in wait for her. And if your voice has a lulling quality to it, that's yet another inducement to relax and drift off, or at least to settle down and settle in. The touch of your free hand—the one not holding the book—can further relax your child. As you rest your hand lightly on his arm as it lies outside the covers, or on his leg through the covers, the feel of your hand is warm and reassuring to him.

But, given all these benefits, you may be wondering, Why do anything other than read a story at night to begin with? If your child still enjoys it when you read a book at bedtime, why look for a different activity to share with her?

- Because sometimes, in order to get relaxed, a child needs a bedtime activity that involves more physical touch than a simple hand on the arm.

- Because some kids—and some parents—enjoy an activity that involves the child more actively than just listening to the parent reading aloud from a book.

- Because no two kids are alike, and some kids simply enjoy an activity more than listening to a book.

- Because while some kids want the same ritual—and even the same story—night after night, other kids enjoy a change of pace.

- Because the parent may welcome the change of pace and be glad to do something different.

- Because some kids will perceive a different settle-down ritual as a treat and will go to bed more willingly when something new and different is offered.

- Because some of the activities in this book, like asking the child what was the best thing that happened to her today, are calculated to get the child thinking happy thoughts, which can help her drift off to sleep more easily.

- Because sometimes you're looking for a quicker activity than reading a whole book, however short, or a whole story from a book of stories. Perhaps your child was late getting to bed because of homework. Maybe you're terribly tired or short of patience tonight. (Parents aren't perfect!) Whatever the reason, you're looking for something to do as you tuck him in that will take only a few minutes, but you don't want to shortchange him altogether and just give him a quick kiss without some kind of settling-down routine.

- Because, conversely, you have more time than usual, and you want to offer your child an additional activity as well as the usual bedtime story.

- Because you may want to encourage the child's creativity in addition to accomplishing your other bedtime objectives. A number of the bedtime activities in this book do that.

So if a story doesn't tempt your child to bed (and even if it does), why not try something else? What you need is an activity—or an assortment of activities to choose from on different nights—that your child can engage in at bedtime, that she'll look forward to, so that she'll be willing to go to bed with that activity in mind. You need activities that will help her calm down, settle down, relax, and get ready to drift off to sleep.

So whether you're tucking in a three-year-old or a nine-year-old, and whether you're tucking in one child, two in one room, or three kids in three separate bedrooms, *Night-Night* offers some activities you can use to help your child settle down and get him ready for sleep.

By the way, my use of *he, him* or *his* in some places in this book, and *she, her,* and *hers* in others is not intended to indicate that some of the bedtime activities I'm talking about are better suited for boys, while others are better for girls. It's simply an attempt to avoid the awkward "he or she" construction, or the gender-neutral but technically ungrammatical "singular 'they.'" All the activities in this book are equally suitable for boys and girls.

Some, however, are better suited to one age than another. Nonetheless, I have purposely not indicated an appropriate age for any of them. One reason for this is that not all kids reach the same level of maturity, capability, or interest at the same age. Some three-year-olds can make up simple stories. Some can't. Some eight-year-olds deem themselves too old for "baby games." Some still enjoy them. And, in fact, at tuck-in time, a familiar ritual may bring great comfort even to a child who has theoretically outgrown it. (Look at the number of otherwise mature kids who still take "blankies" to bed with them.) A few of the activities described in this book require such skills as knowing the alphabet or being able to spell, abilities that don't come to every child at the same age.

So I've made no attempt to indicate a suitable age range for any of these settle-down activities. You know your own child best. You'll probably want to revisit this book every year or so, to be reminded of activities you may have thought were too advanced for your child the last time you read the book. This time around, they may be perfect.

Instead of age categories, I've divided the book into the following parts: Sleepytime Stories; Soothing Games and Quiet Activities; Silly Rhymes, Fun Songs, and Loving Lullabies; and Soft and Gentle Thinking.

And, to go along with the stories, songs, or whatever activity you've chosen for the night, what's more relaxing than a good back rub? You can offer your child a short back rub nightly when she gets into bed, either as a separate activity or even at the same time that you're telling her a story, singing a song to her, or talking to her about her day.

Never underestimate the value of that last nightly contact. It can make all the difference between a peaceful settling-in and a battlefield, or the difference between a successful bedtime and one followed by three reappearances or calls from bed for "Mommmm!" or "Daddyyyyy!"

Use this book well.

Good night, and may you have a peaceful evening.

Sleepytime Stories

Telling a child a bedtime story is a wonderful tradition. But the story doesn't have to be an old childhood favorite. There's nothing wrong with The Three Little Pigs, Charlotte's Web, Robin Hood, or Aladdin . . . to name just a few. But commercial books don't contain the only stories in the world.

The [your family name]s' Own Special Stories

Make up stories to tell your child—stories that no other child gets to hear when she's put to bed at night (and doesn't that make your child feel special?). When I was, oh, maybe ten or eleven, my parents took me to the home of some friends of theirs for dinner. These friends had four children, two of whom were appreciably younger than I was. Their bedtime came while we were still there visiting.

I don't remember how I came to be in the two boys' room when their father was tucking them in; I only remember that, after he had each boy settled into bed, the dad began spinning a tale that he had made up—one I suspect he was making up right then as he went along. It featured (as did many of his stories, as I later learned), a dashing pilot named Harry Heli d'Copter. And, as I also learned, this father appropriated tuck-in time every night—it was always he, not the mom, who saw the boys to bed—and he always told the boys a story of his own invention. Not all the stories featured Harry Heli d'Copter, but all the stories were "Howard Originals."

You can do the same. Of course you don't have to tell an original story *every* night. You can make it a special treat for Sundays, or just whenever inspiration strikes you, and you can tell stories about anyone you want—I'm certainly not suggesting they have to be about a dashing pilot named Harry Heli d'Copter.

You can tell stories involving **adventurers** such as Howard's pilot character, Harry. (Just don't make the stories so exciting that your child gets too keyed up while listening. Remember, your goal is to relax her.) Besides pilots and police, other popular heroes of adventure stories include firefighters, members of the armed forces, and cowboys and cowgirls. (Of course there's no reason your adventure's hero can't be an Everyman, Everywoman, or Everykid who gets caught up in a grand adventure just by happening to be in the right place at the right time.)

You can tell stories about **animals.** Anthropomorphic (having human characteristics) animals have traditionally been a staple of children's stories. And for a child who's facing the first day of kindergarten, a trip to the dentist, or some other potentially scary event, a story about Rudy Rabbit, Harriet Hen, Bert the Bunny, or Betty the Beagle, who has a good visit at the dentist's or a fun time on his first day at school, can be very reassuring.

Of course there are books on such subjects already on the market, but by making up the story yourself, you can tailor it to your child's specific needs, fears, and enjoyments. The animal character can have the same name as your child, or the dentist can have the same name as your child's dentist. The animal can express a specific fear your child holds, and the story can deal with that fear. Or, if your child loves playing with clay, you can have Bert the Bunny discovering that one of the things the kindergarten class does on the first day is play with clay!

Not only will your child enjoy these stories, and not only will he derive a specific benefit from them—reassurance about situations he's facing in his life—but if the story reassures him and relaxes him, he's more likely to be able to go to sleep.

Of course, if you think she's put the trip to the dentist out of her mind for now, that's not the time to remind her by telling a dentist story!

But I don't want you to think that animal stories should deal only with scary or difficult situations. Stories about bunnies going on picnics, goats who have adventures, ducks who want to grow up to be sheep, or horses who wish they had stripes like zebras are always welcome.

The story can have a moral, along the lines of Aesop's fables, though that certainly isn't necessary. A satisfying ending is good enough.

You can make up stories about **kids.** These kids can have believable adventures or fantastic adventures. And, again, the stories can teach a lesson or have a "moral," or they can simply be good, engrossing yarns. They can be about Karen, the seven-year-old detective; or Charley, who befriends the new kid in class when everyone else stays away from him; or Kim, who is the new kid in class. They can be about Rob, who stows away on a rocket to the moon; Melissa, whose fairy godmother gives her a magic stone that makes her invisible when she rubs it; or Joan, who gets to be queen of the world for a day.

The story will be extra-special because you made it up—and you made it up just for your child.

You can make up stories about **your child.** "Kathy Rescues the Princess." "Evan and the Magic Unicorn." (What child doesn't glory in being the star of a story?!) Now the story is not only being made up especially for her, but it's *about* her.

You can tell stories about **people with super-powers,** always a popular theme. The person—adult or child—may have the ability to fly, to make herself invisible, to climb up walls, to jump twenty feet straight up, to jump a block's distance at a time, to hear something that's miles away, to see through walls, or any of the other conventional super-powers. Or you can invent some new super-powers: Maybe he has the ability to project his thoughts in picture form onto a TV screen, or maybe his eyes can send out freezing rays that will instantly turn milk and syrup into ice cream! Maybe she can freeze people, so that bad guys trying to get away from her are turned instantly to ice or concrete. (What new super-powers can *you* think up?)

You can even ask your child what superpowers he would like the hero or heroine of your story to have.

And, of course, if your child enjoys the first story, you can make up a whole string of adventures starring the same super-power-possessing hero. Just as my parents' friend Howard told his boys many adventures starring Harry Heli d'Copter, you too can have a recurring character who populates many of your stories.

You can tell stories about existing **popular characters:**

"The New Adventures of Robin Hood"

"The Seven Dwarfs Find a New Friend"

"An Eighth Dwarf Joins the Group"

"Santa's New Reindeer"

"The Night Rudolph's Nose Stopped Glowing"

"The Three Little Pigs and the Wolf's Hungry Cousin"

"Cinderella's Children"

"The Tooth Fairy's Bad Night"

You can even play mix 'n' match with characters:

"Snow White Meets Hansel and Gretel"

"Rapunzel Climbs Jack's Beanstalk"

"Santa Claus Visits the Land of Oz"

In short, you can make up stories on almost any subject. Your only limits are your own imagination and your child's level of comprehension.

Turnabout Is Fair Play

Have the child tell you a story! Now, there's a switch . . .
but it's a fun one. Little kids will probably just retell an old
familiar favorite, "Sleeping Beauty" or "Red Riding Hood"
or "Cinderella." But as they get older, kids' imaginations
become better equipped to construct stories, and with a little encouragement, your Sean can be spinning tales with
the best of them.

Again, as I said about stories you make up, he can always make up a new adventure for an old familiar character, whether it's Winnie the Pooh or Peter Rabbit or the
Ugly Duckling. (Kids a little older may pick comic book
characters as the heroes of their stories.) But after he gets
comfortable with making up stories about familiar characters, encourage him to make up totally original stories if
he can. Why not foster his creativity while you're settling
him in for the night?

And if he finds a character he likes, encourage him to
tell more stories on other nights about that boy, that super-
powered woman, that lonely skunk, or that apprentice
witch.

Tune in Tomorrow, for the Next Exciting Episode!

Unless you're a whiz at storytelling, this one will probably require a little advance planning, but it's worth the effort. You can tell your child a serial story, one that has a new installment every night. To do this, you don't just make up a story; you make up one that continues in nightly installments.

This isn't all that different from reading a book to your child, one chapter each night, but ideally, you'll leave off each night's installment in a "cliffhanger" place in the story. Now your child will have an extra reason for being willing to go to bed—the sooner he lets you tuck him in, the sooner he can hear what happened next to Jimmy (or Joanne, or Professor Heimelweiner, or Denny the Dragon).

Last night, Jimmy had just found those huge footprints. Oh boy! He thought for sure the footprints had to have been made by a dinosaur! Was he really about to find a real live dinosaur in the forest? Or would it turn out that something else had left those giant imprints in the forest floor . . . and if so, what? What else could have made footprints that huge?

If your child wants to find out, she'd better get in bed quickly. There won't be any story till her teeth are brushed, her pajamas are on, she's gone to the bathroom, and whatever else she needs to do is done.

Of course, if you can't make up stories yourself, you can always serialize a long story from a book, but it's so much more fun when you write the story yourself . . . and your child can't cheat and ask a friend, during the day, if he knows how the story ends.

ell a Tall Tale

Tall tales are stories that you know could never really have happened but are told as if they are true. If your child has read or heard any of the legends of Paul Bunyan, Mike Fink, or Pecos Bill, he knows what a tall tale is.

Kids love making up tall tales, and especially when the kids themselves are the heroes of the tales. Why not let your child tell tall tales about himself some nights at bedtime? Whether the story concerns a trip to Mars on a rocket, or chopping down a tree with a kitchen knife, rescuing her best friend from a monster and being declared an Official Hero, or sailing across the country on a cloud, she can let his imagination soar . . . and tell lies with impunity.

Telling tall tales is tall fun!

The Chains That Bind

Engage in a "chain story" with your child. He tells a little bit of the story and then stops. Now it's your turn. You tell some more of the story, but stop before you get carried away and tell the whole thing. Now it's his turn again.

If you're putting two kids to bed in the same room at the same time, all three of you can take turns with the story. You tell a little, then turn the story over to Danny, who tells a little more and turns the story over to Ron. When Ron has told part of the story, it's your turn again, and so on.

It's best when you can stop your segment just at a "cliffhanger part" of the story. "Sharon turned the corner, and she was amazed at what she saw!" And then tell your child, "Okay, it's your turn to tell the story. What did Sharon see?" Or, "The door to the room swung shut, and Heather realized she was trapped inside. How was she going to get out? Then she realized a way she could do it. . . . Okay, it's your turn. How did Heather get out?"

The story is over when it comes to a logical conclusion, when the child loses interest, or when he falls asleep.

Alpha Bet They'll Love This One!

Similar to chain stories are alphabet stories. These, too, involve each player adding to the story in turn, in this case one sentence at a time, but here you're bound by the letters of the alphabet—if the first player's sentence starts with *L*, the second player's sentence must start with *M*, and then, as the game comes back to the first player, she must offer a sentence that begins with *N*.

Of course, if you're putting two kids to bed at one time, and there are three players, you, Brian, and Seth, and you lead off with a sentence beginning with *L*, Brian's sentence would start with *M*, Seth's would start with *N*, and then it's back to you for *O*.

Notes:

- You can start the game with a sentence beginning with any letter. It doesn't have to begin with A.

- You may decide in advance to omit any of the problematic letters—such as *X*, most likely, and perhaps *Q* and/or *Z*.

After the sentence beginning with Z (or, if you've de-cided to omit Z, then after the sentence beginning with Y), circle around to A.

The game is over when you get back to the letter you started with (unless the child falls asleep before that, of course!).

There is no winner or loser—the game is not competitive.

Silly sentences are welcome. For a story beginning with *L*, you might start, "Llamas with purple polka dots were marching at the head of the parade down Main Street."

Because you don't have to start with *A* every time you play, your child is less likely to fall into a rut by telling a similar-themed story every time. (And, of course, *you* can lead off the story, gently guiding her into a differ-ent scenario.)

● It's a game, not an attempt to win the Nobel Prize for literature, so if the story wanders, changes focus, or has some other literary flaw, don't worry about it.

🌙 Obviously, this is a game for kids who know their alphabet and can spell well enough to know what letter a word starts with.

Sleepytime
Stories

25

"Tell Me a Mommy Story"

Tell your child a true story from your childhood. Kids love hearing that mommies and daddies were once little kids themselves. It's a fascinating concept. In a little child's mind, Mommy was always a mommy, or at least a grown woman, and Daddy was always a daddy, or at least a grown man. And even after kids finally grasp the concept that Mommy and Daddy were once little kids themselves, there's still a whole other concept to grasp: that the world was different then, that many of the things your child takes for granted didn't exist, or were different, back then.

Maybe you didn't have a computer, or maybe you had a computer but no e-mail. You probably played some of the same games your child plays, when you were her age—Hide 'n' Seek, or Tag, You're It!—but you probably played different ones too.

Talk about your childhood, and the ways in which the world was different then, especially for a kid. (You know that kids enjoy best hearing what they can relate to themselves.) Talk about the things that were the same, too, but may be things your child never thought of your ever having done. Did you have to go to the doctor for shots? Did you cry? Did you have a best friend? Were you the reigning jump rope champ on your block, or the marbles king? Did you have the biggest comic book collection of all your friends? Or the strictest parents? Or the funniest uncle? Or a grandma who baked the best cookies? Did you have a mean older brother, who picked on you, or a little sister whom you helped take care of? Did you and your sister fight over who got to lick the bowl when your mom baked cookies? Did you get into trouble for sneaking cookies you weren't supposed to have?

Tell about your first day in school. Tell how you spent your summers. Tell about your best friend and the things you liked to do together. Tell about your pets. Tell about your first two-wheeler . . . or even your first tricycle, if you remember that far back. Tell your child the ways in which your childhood was like hers . . . and the ways in which it was different.

Did you live in a house or an apartment? Or maybe you lived in someplace different—a trailer or military housing, for instance. Perhaps a farmhouse. What was the best thing about the house you grew up in? What was the worst? Did you have to share your room with a brother or sister?

Who was your favorite neighbor? Who did you like the least of all the people you knew? Why? Who was your favorite teacher? Why? What was your best subject in school? What were your favorite toys? How did you celebrate your birthdays? What were your parties like?

There are many stories you can tell about your childhood, and they don't have to be adventures. They can just be simple, quiet reminiscences. Your child will enjoy hearing them . . . and you'll probably enjoy telling them, as well.

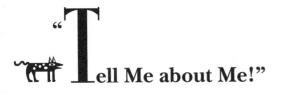

"Tell Me about Me!"

While you're telling stories of childhoods past, tell your child about her own younger years. "When you were really little" is a popular topic for kids. For a nine-year-old, stories of when she was four or five may recall events she's forgotten, or tell her things she simply doesn't remember at all. For a three-year-old, "when you were really little" pretty much means "when you were a baby" or a toddler. But little kids love hearing stories about themselves. The story of how and where she took her first step, or a description of her first birthday may fascinate her no matter how many times she hears it. Kids old enough to understand the birth process love to hear about the day or night they were born.

Picture This Story

For this story-game, you need to do a bit of advance preparation. Cut out some pictures from magazines. They should be primarily pictures of things, rather than of people. If they are of people, they shouldn't be just generic ones, but rather specific types such as football players, firefighters, police officers, doctors, or teachers. Other pictures might be of airplanes, cars, trains, or buses; snow, rain, or clouds; houses, schools, or office buildings; dogs, cats, elephants, tigers, or other animals; toys; pots and pans, utensils, or plates; furniture; watches or clocks; or most anything else that a child will readily recognize. It's fine if these pictures are cut out of advertisements.

If you plan on playing this story-game frequently, you may want to glue each picture to a piece of cardboard to make them more durable.

When you're ready to play, turn the pictures upside down (back side up, not head to toe), shuffle them, and offer them to your child. She needs to pick any five without knowing what they are. When she's done this, she turns them over to see what five pictures she has.

She now needs to make up a story that involves all five pictures. It can include anyone and anything else that she wants, in addition.

With a young child, or one with an underdeveloped imagination, the "story" may be very short. If she drew out a picture of an elephant, a doctor, a firefighter, a ball, and some trees, she might tell a story as simple and brief as: Once there was an elephant who got sick. She lay down under a tree at the zoo and wouldn't play with the ball that the zookeeper gave her. The zookeeper called the doctor, and he made her better. A firefighter came to the zoo, and the elephant was feeling better, and the firefighter looked at her, and she stood up again and he fed her peanuts. The End.

On the other hand, an older child, or one with a more developed imagination, might spin a long yarn involving a doctor's office that catches fire, and an elephant who helps put out the fire by spraying water on the fire through her trunk. The tree and ball will find their way into the story too, somewhere along the way.

The story may not win the Caldecott Medal, but it will

be fun for your child (and good for stretching her "imagination muscles").

If the story she writes is short, return the five pictures to the group, reshuffle, and let her draw five again and make up another story. If she has told a longer yarn, and it's well and truly bedtime now, kiss her goodnight.

Night-Night

Mirror Story

Can your child repeat a story you've told her? Can she improve on it?

Tell your child a story, preferably one she's not familiar with. Then ask her to repeat the story to you. If you wish, tell her she's free to alter it, improve on it, even change the ending.

It will be interesting to see how your story sounds when she repeats it back to you. Whether or not you encourage her to make changes, it will be interesting to see what changes she makes, whether intentionally or as a result of her not remembering it perfectly.

White, White, Say Good Night

If you tell your child a story with soothing images, the mental picture can help lull her to sleep. And what is more neutral, soothing, and calming than a vast landscape of white? Tell your child a story that will have her envisioning a world of vast white landscapes. A fellow writer suggests the following outline for a story. For a three-year-old, you might not have to add many details; for older kids, you'll need to build on this framework and insert some adventures and excitement as the sheep make their roundabout way home. Here's the story outline:

Some white, white sheep were walking home across a frosty meadow when a fog came up. Unable to see their way, they followed the sweet smells of the barn to find their way home, but then it began to snow. Along the way, they met a snowman (insert some adventure or excitement here), wandered off track and encountered a polar bear (insert some more excitement or happenings), but finally got directed back to their barn. There they were greeted by Lily, the white collie. Finally they entered the white,

snow-covered barn to find Puff, the
white kitten, playing with a white ball
of yarn on the whitewashed floor. After
eating some white Cream of Wheat for
supper, they settled down and snuggled
up to one another with Puff and Lily for
a long winter's nap.

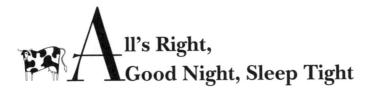

All's Right, Good Night, Sleep Tight

Along the line of soothing stories, how about getting your child to make up a bedtime story . . . about bedtime? This can be a story of you (or his other parent) tucking him in, or a story about another child going to bed, or about a mama bunny or cow, robin, or sheep tucking her child in.

The story may have a complex plot or very little substance; it doesn't matter. Since the child is making it up himself, it will amuse him regardlessly. And since it's a story about bedtime, a story in which someone is being put to bed, it will put him in mind of . . . ho-hum . . . *yawwwwwn* . . . going to sleep.

Recap Nightcap

Sometimes all it takes to put a child in a good place in his head is to get him to reflect on the best thing that happened to him that day. And sometimes the easiest way to get her to do that is to just *ask* her, "What was the best thing that happened today, honey?"

For some parents, this may seem like a good idea for *every* night—and for some kids, it will be. For other parents, this may seem like a good idea to employ occasionally . . . perhaps when you know your child has something especially good to look back on, or when you know your child is most in need of some happy-making thoughts, or when you know that thinking back on the day isn't likely to raise some *other* thoughts besides the best-of ones, thoughts you had better leave as far away as possible if you want sleep to come calling quickly.

Another point to consider: Some kids are likely to reply to this question—even on what's been a banner day—with half a sentence at best. Other kids may go on remembering aloud till it's long past lights-out time.

But whether you get your child to recall the best thing about his day nightly, semi-regularly, or only occasionally, whether he's the sort who's likely to answer the question in three words or twenty minutes, there's probably some place for it in your roster of bedtime activities.

Recap Nightcap: The Illustrated Version

Does your child like to draw? Can she draw a "finished" picture in about ten or fifteen minutes (so that bedtime isn't postponed an hour by this activity)? Instead of asking her to *tell you* about the best thing that happened to her today (see previous activity), you can ask her to *draw a picture* of it.

Again, this may be an every-night activity for some kids, a once-in-a-blue-moon activity for others, and something in between for still other kids.

To make it feasible that your child can draw while in bed, I'm assuming that either he has a night table that can double as a drawing surface, he has a big book with a flat surface that you don't mind his leaning on to draw, or that some other simple arrangement presents itself that facilitates his drawing in bed. I'm also assuming he's not one of those fussy artists who insists on using the large box of crayons and having each one laid out neatly in plain view on the drawing surface while he works.

Of course, he can tell you the story he's drawing, too . . . while he draws it, beforehand, or afterward, to explain what he's drawn.

Soothing Games and Quiet Activities

Although you don't want to engage your child in a game that's going to make him rambunctious or get him mentally excited in his zeal to win, quiet games have a place at bedtime. These games can be designed to induce relaxation, or they can even be mildly competitive. The prospect of playing a game with Mommy or Daddy is a good inducement for getting into bed. And there's nothing wrong with a game at bedtime, provided it's one that can be played lying down, quietly, and without getting the child all geared up again.

A round the World in Bed

If your child is old enough to be able to spell, the Geography game is a fine choice for bedtime. You may remember this game from your own childhood or play it with your child already, but in case neither of these is so, here's a quick refresher course:

The first player names any place name—city, state, country, continent, even a body of water. (No, wise guy . . . the bathtub doesn't count!) The next player must name another place, one whose name begins with the letter the last place name ended with. For instance, if you said, "Indiana," which ends with *A*, your child must name a place beginning with *A*—perhaps "Africa." Okay, that's an *A* back to you, and if you say, "Akron," he now has to come up with a place beginning with an *N*—such as "New Orleans," "North America," "New York," or "North Carolina."

Of course, if you're putting two kids to bed at one time in the same room, and both are old enough to spell somewhat competently, all three of you can play. If you lead off, and Allison follows, Hillary follows Allison, and you follow Hillary.

No repetitions are allowed. A place that's been named once in the game may not be used again. A player who repeats is not out of the game, but that answer isn't accepted, and he has to think of a different one. When a player is stumped and cannot think of a new place name beginning with the requisite letter, then he's out of the game. The last player left is the winner.

Getting Bedtimes "Licked"

Here's a very simple game for younger players, accompanied by stroking motions meant to soothe and relax the child and help him get to sleep. It's not the sort of game that has an object to it; it's not competitive; it's just a little ritual meant to lull the child into a relaxed state.

Start by saying, "There's a friendly dog licking your right arm." As you say it, stroke softly and soothingly along his arm. Next say, "There's a friendly dog licking your left arm," and stroke softly and soothingly along his other arm. These strokes should be calm, soft, and slow, not exciting, inducing a drowsy, easy, relaxed state.

Continue with, "There's a friendly dog licking your side," "There's a friendly dog licking your chest," "There's a friendly dog licking your left leg," and so on. You can add his feet, or mention the thigh and calf separately, if you wish. End with, "There's a friendly dog licking your head," and stroke his head.

Be sure to avoid any place where you know he's ticklish.

Are You Having N-U-F?

How well can your child spell . . . backward? If she's a competent enough speller to spell at least simple words forward confidently, challenge her to spell backward! You can offer such simple challenges as *cat* and *fun,* or longer words, such as *play* or even *school.*

Comic Indeed!

What child old enough to read doesn't love comic books? And what child doesn't at one time or another have aspirations of drawing them himself?

If your child is old enough to write, he can be encouraged to draw a comic book. It may be of the humorous variety (think *Archie*) or the adventure sort (think *Spiderman*).

The "book" may be only two pages or just a few panels; your child may even have to ask you how to spell every other word. But the important thing is that he's creating something of his own, he's involved in a project that fosters creativity, he's doing something that encourages him to write, and at bedtime, when you tuck him in, he can proudly read his comic book to you, taking great pleasure in his creation. (And what will make a child go to sleep more happily than a feeling of swelling pride?)

Never mind that his pictures may all be stick figures, that his Octopusman's super-powers bear a strong resemblance to those of Superman, or that most of the words are misspelled. It's his. He created it. And as he shows it off and reads it to you, he can bask in a happy haze of creativity and drift off to sleep very satisfied with himself.

Hand-y for Talking

Entertain your child with finger conversations. What are
finger conversations? Why, they're conversations your right
index finger has with your left index finger, of course!
Hold your two hands up in fists facing each other, and
raise your two index fingers. As your right index finger is
supposed to be talking, wiggle it; when your left index
finger is supposedly answering, wiggle
that finger.

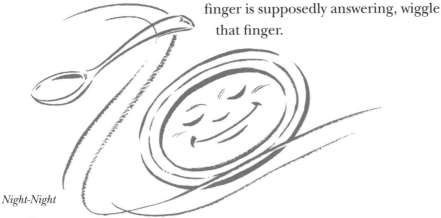

Night-Night

48

And do use different voices for the two fingers. You may want to use an exaggeratedly high voice for one finger and an exaggeratedly low voice for the other, or a growly voice for one and a sweet voice for the other, or in some other exaggerated way differentiate the two fingers vocally.

What are your fingers going to talk about? That's up to you. You can have them talk about something as simple as the weather, or you can have each one talking about a day in school or a day at work—whether your fingers are kids, grownups, or one of each is entirely up to you. You can even delight your child by having your fingers talk about him!

The conversation doesn't have to be long, fascinating, or brilliant. It will amuse a small child anyhow, if you just use your imagination in the conversation.

Easy, Breezy Finger Puppets

Akin to the talking fingers are finger puppets. Here's a really easy way to put faces on your fingers in no time flat, followed by a sleep-inducing routine your finger puppets can go through whenever you want.

First, instructions for the faces:

Take two Band-Aids out of their wrappers and lay them down horizontally. With a pen or fine line marker, draw a rudimentary face on the back of the pad of each Band-Aid. Now put on one Band-Aid near the tip of each of your index fingers. Make sure the faces are in the right place and right side up! When you point your fingers upward, the faces should be upright and on the front (the pad, or fingerprint side) of each finger, so that when your fists are facing each other, with index fingers upraised, the faces are facing each other too.

Now make a fist of each hand, then point only the index fingers up into the air. Hold your fists facing each other, a few inches apart. As you sit on the bed alongside your child, hold your hands so that he can see both faces. As with the activity above, when each finger is "talking," wiggle it slightly. And as with the activity above, use a markedly different voice for each finger.

Now, what are the two fingers going to talk to each other about? About bedtime!

RIGHT FINGER: It's bedtime.

LEFT FINGER: Is it bedtime all over?

RF: Yes.

LF: Is it bedtime on the farm?

RF: It's bedtime on the farm.

LF: Are the sheep all asleep?

RF: The sheep are all asleep.

LF: Are the cows all asleep?

RF: The cows are all asleep.

LF: Are the chickens all asleep?

RF: The chickens are all asleep.

LF: Are the pigs all asleep?

RF: The pigs are all asleep.

LF: Is it bedtime in the city?

RF: It's bedtime in the city.

LF: Are the city kids going to sleep?

RF: The city kids are going to sleep.

LF: Is it bedtime for Jeremy? [Replace "Jeremy" with your child's name]

RF: It's bedtime for Jeremy.

LF: Is Jeremy going to sleep?

RF: Jeremy will soon be asleep.

LF: Good night, cows.

RF: Good night, sheep.

LF: Good night, chickens.

RF: Good night, pigs.

LF: Good night, city kids.

RF: Good night, Jeremy.

LF: Good night, Jeremy.

YOU (in your own voice): Good night, honey.

Of course, you can have a different conversation going on between your two fingers than the one above. If your child tires of the same dialogue but not of the finger puppets, write a new conversation for them—preferably one that still reinforces the idea that it's bedtime.

# Stick It to Me!

Instead of Band-Aid puppets, you can make simple stick puppets if you'd like. Cut two pictures of people out of magazines (ads are fine for this). Humorous drawings are better than photographs, but either will do. The pictures should be of similar size to each other. It's better if they're not of recognizably famous people, but it's good if they're of identifiable types—for example, a grandma, a babysitter, a police officer, or a firefighter are good, though generic men or women (or kids) are fine too.

Paste the two pictures to a piece of cardboard, then cut around the figures. Now glue each cut-out figure to a Popsicle stick or a wooden pencil (not a round one but one with flat sides).

If you want, you can cut out more than two figures and have different puppets put your child to bed on different nights.

You can have these puppets perform the same dialogue, or a similar one as is given for the Band-Aid puppets, or write your own dialogue, or just let the puppets have a conversation with your child. The advantage to the conversation given for the Band-Aid puppets, besides the fact that it has strong suggestions of bedtime, is that many kids like routine, and while some will tire quickly of the same dialogue, others will relish the nightly familiarity.

You know your own child best. You know whether to use the same dialogue every night, use it often but vary it with other bedtime routines, or skip it in favor of something more spontaneous that the puppets can say to him.

Good Night, Teddy

Just as you put your child to bed, your child can put her favorite bear, doll, toy dog, or other stuffed playmate to bed. Whether Teddy has a special resting place for the night, the doll has a cradle of her own, the toy dog sleeps in bed with your child, or she merely puts her toy elephant down on the floor and kisses him good night, if she "tucks him in," kisses him, murmurs soothing words to him, and perhaps even sings a lullabye to him, she'll be putting herself in the right frame of mind for sleep too.

And Now for the News . . .

What's the news of the day? On the *real* TV, they may be talking of battles, politics, the economy, and other such weighty matters. On your child's pretend TV, the news is more likely about spelling tests, fun (or fights) with your child's best friend, the mystery meat in the school lunch, and other such . . . well, weighty matters.

Suggest that when your child gets into bed, he should sit there and deliver the news, TV newscaster-style. If you usually watch the 5:00 or 6:00 news, he's likely been exposed to the format of a news broadcast, and if he's old enough, he can probably do a reasonable imitation of your favorite national or local news anchor.

He'll enjoy the fun of sounding important . . . and you just might learn something he didn't bother to tell you when he came home, too eager to eat a snack and play to report on his day in school. Perhaps your "How was school?" elicited merely "Fine," and your, "What happened today?" got a "Nothing" in return. Now's your chance to get the *real* scoop!

Silly Fill-ins

There's a popular copyrighted game for two or more players that's been around for a couple of generations now, involving filling in the blanks in a story with one part of speech or another. But you don't have to buy the preprinted version—you can make up your own stories. Here's how to prepare and how to play.

Note that this is only for kids old enough to know the parts of speech: A child needs to know what a noun, verb, adverb, and adjective are in order to play this.

To prepare, write a short story—just two or three paragraphs. But leave some of the words out. For instance, you might write:

> One day, [name of person] got into the bathtub with his/her [toy]. S/he took the soap and washed himself/herself in [number] places. S/he used so much soap that the bubbles went clear to [a building].
>
> S/he yelled, "Holy [animal]! I'd better let the water out of the [noun] before I [verb]." S/he got out of the tub and

dried himself/herself, went into his/her room and put on
clean [noun]s.

    Then she called up [person] on the [noun] and said,
"Come over right away and look at my [adjective] bathtub.
You won't believe how tall the [noun]s are."

Got the idea? One more thing: Leave room to write in
the words your child will give you when you ask him for a
name, noun, or other part of speech.

Now, to play: Hold the story so your child can't see it.
Ask him for a noun, a verb, a name, a number, an adjective, a toy . . . whatever the blanks require. Write his answer
down. When he's filled in all the blanks, read back the entire story, with the words he's given you to fill in the blanks
with.

The Name Game

My daughter and her friends used to swear that the car make "FORD" stood for Found On Road Dead. With a little bit of thought, your child can come up with appropriate phrases for her friends' names, too. (No cruelty, please!)

Of course she needs to be able to spell well enough to know what letter each word starts with; clearly this isn't an activity for four-year-olds. But if she's old enough to be a halfway decent speller, she can engage in this fun pastime. The letters don't have to stand for something *about the person:* KAYLA could translate to Kangaroos Are Young Leaping Acrobats, though BOB could certainly be interpreted as Bright Or Brilliant.

Just Call Me "Paper"

A fun diversion for kids old enough to know their alphabet, and possibly to spell, is "back-writing." No, not backward-writing . . . back-writing.

If your child is wearing flannel PJs, this may not work as well, but cotton (or other thin) PJs, or a bare back, will easily allow for you to take your index finger and trace a large capital letter on his back. Now he has to decide which letter you've "written" on his back.

For kids who know more than just their alphabet—kids who can spell whole words—you can write not just one letter but a whole word. Don't attempt to write small as if actually printing the letters side by side across her back. Print the first letter, using large strokes, in the middle of her back. Then pause, or pat her back, or say "next letter"—anything to signal that you have finished the first letter—and, in the same space in the middle of her back, print the next letter. Continue in this manner until you've spelled out the whole word.

Unless the child in question is a ten-year-old spelling whiz, confine your choice of words to short, familiar ones—if not as simplistic as *dog*, at least perhaps *house*, rather than *backyard* or *question*.

Show-Offs Shine

Let your child show off his numbers skills. Have him count as high as he can, or count by twos, by fives, or by tens. Or let him count backward from 100. For a slightly older child, give him more of a challenge and ask him to count by sixes or sevens, or count backward by fives.

Regardless of how well he does, praise him either for achievement or for trying.

I'm Blue

A gentle game with no winners or losers . . . more along the lines of a challenge to your child . . . is to ask her how many things he can think of that have a certain characteristic. For instance, you might ask, "How many blue things can you think of?" Other possible questions include,

- How many green things can you think of in your room?

- How many things in the kitchen can you think of that begin with the letter *S?*

- How many rectangular things can you think of in the house?

- How many wooden things can you think of in the house that aren't furniture?

- How many things can you think of in the living room that are smaller than a shoebox?

- How many things can you think of in the house that we have two or more of?

Don't Deliver This Letter!

Another quiet game is Forbidden Letter. To play this, you state a letter and ask a question. For example, you might say, "*H*. What did you do after school?" Your child now needs to answer the question *in at least six words* and *without using the "forbidden letter"*—in this case, *H*. The answer does not need to be truthful, but it does need to be responsive to the question.

Your child cannot answer, "Homework," for two reasons: It's only one word, and it contains the forbidden letter. She can't answer, "I'm going to see my grandma next week," because it's not responsive to the question. But she could say, "I went over to my grandma's." Never mind that Grandma lives in Milwaukee and your child hasn't seen her in six months; the answer was at least six words long, was responsive to the question, and didn't contain the forbidden letter.

Of course she can turn the tables and make you answer a question next, without using the forbidden letter (which need not be *H* this time around).

Seizin' the Season 🐍

The Game of the Seasons is a fun little card game that's suitable even for kids who can't yet read. They don't even have to know their numbers. You'll need to create the card deck yourself, so a little pre-bedtime prep is in order. Here's what you need to do:

One set of seasons cards consists of four cards, each depicting a tree during one of the seasons. The "winter" card shows the tree with its branches bare of any leaves. The "spring" card shows the tree's branches with small green dots, representing the budding leaves of spring. The "summer" card shows the tree in full leaf. And the "autumn" card shows the tree's leaves in the riotous colors of autumn.

Your child can make the cards himself, perhaps with a little parental help in cutting the cardboard you'll probably use to create the cards on. All the cards should be the same size, of course.

If you and one child are playing, you will need three sets of seasons cards. If you are putting two kids to bed at once and playing this with them both, you will need four sets of cards. In other words, you always need *one more set* of cards than there are players.

Now, here's how to play:

Shuffle together all the cards you are using (remember, one set for each player plus one extra set) and place the shuffled deck face down on the playing surface (probably your child's bed). The first player—let's say that's your child—draws one card and puts it face up in front of herself. The next player does the same.

Assuming you are playing with one child, play now returns to the first player. She draws the top card from the face-down draw pile and looks at it. The player needs a card that depicts the season following the one shown on the card previously drawn. Let's say the first card she drew was autumn. She is now looking for a winter card. If the second card drawn is a winter card, she lays it down next to her autumn card. If the second card drawn is anything other than the one she needs, however, she places it in a face-up discard pile next to the face-down draw pile.

Now it's the second player's turn. Let's say the first card you drew was a spring card. You need a summer card now. You do the same thing your child did—draw the top card from the face-down draw pile and look at it. If it's the summer card, you put it down face up, next to your spring card on the playing surface. Otherwise you discard it face up in the discard pile.

Play now returns to the first player. Play continues to alternate (or to go around in a circle in the case of a three-player game), with players drawing cards, putting them face up in front of them if the cards follow sequentially the cards they already have, and discarding them otherwise.

It is highly unlikely that anyone will complete his four-season layout before the draw pile is exhausted. When there are no cards left in the draw pile, turn the discard pile upside down, shuffle it, and use it for a new draw pile. Do this as often as you need to till a player wins the game.

The first player to get all four seasons in order is the winner.

(Of course, more than two can play, too. While two or three players are the most you're likely to have at bedtime, if you have three kids and want to play this game with all of them at some other time, or if your child has four friends visiting him one day and wants to play this game with them, there's no reason it won't work with any number of players. Just make sure you have the required number of card sets.)

Do a Number on Your Child

For a child old enough to know most of the answers, a numbers quiz (call it a "game" so it doesn't sound like schoolwork!) will give her a chance to show off how smart she is. The questions you ask can be as simple as, "How many pennies in a nickel?" or "How many fingers on each hand?" or they can be more difficult for an older child.

Here are some questions to get you started:

- How many stars in the flag?
- How many states in the United States?
- How many stars in the Big Dipper?
- How many players on a baseball team?
- How many ounces in a pound?
- How many inches in a foot?
- How many toes do four people have altogether?
- How many nickels equal a quarter?

☽ [For older kids:] How many pennies equal two dimes, two nickels and a quarter?

☿ How many digits in a phone number (with/without the area code)?

☾ How many eggs in a container?

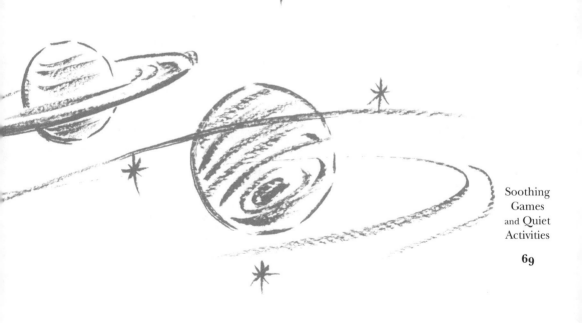

Hide 'n' Seek . . . and Stay Put!

Have you ever played Hide 'n' Seek in your mind . . . without actually secreting yourself in a hidden spot? That's what you and your child will do when you play Where Is Karen (substitute your child's name here) Hiding? It's a combination of Hide 'n' Seek and Hot and Cold . . . and it's all done mentally!

First your child picks a place in the house that she imagines herself hiding in. You should decide in advance whether this needs to be a place she could access in real life and realistically fit into, or whether you'll allow silly, unrealistic hiding places. You also need to decide if any place is off limits (for instance, you may want to rule out dangerous places, so that she doesn't try really hiding in the oven in a real game of Hide 'n' Seek at a later date), or if, to keep the game short, you want to restrict the game to certain rooms, or to one floor of the house, or otherwise limit the hiding area.

When she's mentally picked a hiding place, she calls out, "Ready!" and you start by saying, "Where is Karen hiding?" Then you say, "I think I'll look in ____ first," naming a room—Karen's room, Brian's room, the living room, the kitchen.

Now she has to answer, "Hot," "Cold," or "Warm," according to how close you are to her hiding place. (If you've picked the right room, she'd say, "Hot." If you've picked a room near where she's hiding, she'd say, "Warm." If you've picked a room at the wrong end of a big house, or on the wrong floor of a multi-floor house, she'd say, "Cold.")

If you're in the wrong room, you say, "I'm walking out into the hall. I'm turning left" (or "I'm turning toward the front of the house," or "I'm turning toward Brian's room"). She then answers "Warmer," or "Cooler," or "Still cold," or other temperature clues as appropriate.

When you get to the right room, she may not want to give clues as you walk around the room; this would make it much easier, perhaps too easy. She may want only to say, "Hot," "Cool," or "Warmer," or "Cooler," as you look in a closet, under a bed, or whatever other opportunities that room offers. When you finally find her, she announces she's been found—no cheating and denying it—and the game's over.

If the game was over too quickly—or the next night, as a variation—*you* can hide and she can try to find you.

You Do the Hokey Pokey and You Get Yourself in Bed

I'm sure you know the hokey pokey song:

> You put your right foot in,
> You take your right foot out,
> You put your right foot in,
> And you shake it all about.
> You do the Hokey Pokey and you turn yourself around.
> That's what it's all about!

(Repeat this verse for the right leg, left foot, left leg, body, right hand, right arm, left hand, and left arm.)

Your child can go to bed to the tune of the hokey pokey! Start with him standing next to the bed, his side to the bed's side. If his left leg is nearer to the bed, start with the left leg; his right leg is nearer, you'll start with his right leg.

Start the game, like the song, with the first foot. When you sing about putting the right foot in, he raises his right foot and slips it under the covers, taking it out again, of course, on the next line. On the line about shaking it about, he merely wriggles his right foot; you don't want to get him so active that he's wide awake again. On the line about doing the hokey pokey, he gently wriggles his whole body. Instead of singing, "And you turn yourself around," sing, "And you get beneath the sheet." "That's what it's all about" becomes "That's how you go to bed."

The verse is now repeated for his right leg. When you sing about putting his right leg in, he moves his tushy onto the bed and slides his right leg under the covers. When you sing about taking it out, he withdraws his leg only as far as the foot; that remains under the covers.

Now comes his left foot, and then his left leg (or, if he's started with his left side, he puts his right foot and leg under the covers now).

The next verse is his body. Then left (or right) hand, then arm, then the other hand, then arm.

And that's all. He's in bed. Good night!

Riddled with Smiles

Riddles amuse kids, usually without sending them into gales of laughter, so they're a good activity for bedtime too. (The classic kid riddle is, What has four wheels and flies? Answer: A garbage truck.) The quiet enjoyment of a riddle works both ways—whether you ask the riddles or whether your child does. (There's no reason your bedtime riddle session can't feature some of each.)

If your child is still quite young, some of her riddles may strike you as not particularly funny—but this is about getting your child to sleep, not about winning a talent show. As long as she's getting quiet enjoyment, don't worry if her riddles are less than funny or don't make perfect sense. She'll improve with time. Right now the important thing is that she settles down in bed.

Calendar Countdown

Does your child look forward to the activities of the next day? Does she get a reassured feeling that nothing scary is waiting for her then? One mother I know of has a calendar just for her child. Each evening, the child watches Mom mark off the day just gone by on the calendar; then they discuss the next day ahead.

What does it hold? Is there a trip to someplace special in store? Some other treat? After the rest of the evening's ritual (in their case, bath, vitamins, prayers, and a story), they look at the calendar together. Then they reconstruct the day gone by, discussing the day's events, and look ahead to what's scheduled for the next day.

If there's nothing scheduled that should concern the child, she gets the reassurance of knowing this. If there's a visit to the doctor or dentist, or anything else that might be cause for any worry on her part, she may already have known this even before being told that it's on the calendar. By being given the opportunity to talk about her concerns now, she can get the reassurance she needs.

When she's done talking out the things that may perturb her, she can snuggle down and go to sleep.

Of course I don't recommend this for major worrywarts and/or for kids who don't already know that a doctor's visit is on tap for tomorrow. Neither do I endorse it for kids who can bounce off the ceiling with joy and unabated excitement just to hear that Aunt Pam is visiting tomorrow.

But is your child the sort who is more upset when a dentist visit catches her by surprise than when she knows in advance, even if advance warning leads to brooding and worrying about it? If so, then this is a fine way to talk out her concerns.

And the majority of nights, when there's nothing on tap for tomorrow but the playground, or a playdate with a friend, or a plan for you and her to bake cookies together, this is a lovely way to get her to bed all set up for good times ahead tomorrow.

Alpha-Journeys

Can your child name an animal, fish, or bird that begins with *A* . . . *B* . . . *C* . . . *D* . . . ? For how many letters of the alphabet can he think of a person he knows (friend, relative, neighbor—include fictional characters too, if you want, or make that the subject of yet another challenge)? Challenge your child to work his way through the alphabet thinking of a name, an animal, a growing thing (trees, bushes, flowers, plants), a food, a place, or any other category you can devise, for each letter of the alphabet that he can.

This isn't competitive nor is it a school test, so feel free to help him when he gets stuck. (You can give him hints or even contribute an answer outright.) There may not be a bird or fish that starts with *X*, or a person he knows whose name starts with *Q*, so make sure he understands that if he doesn't come up with an answer, he has neither lost nor failed. There are no points awarded in this gentle activity, nor is it a win/lose situation.

The only winner is your child, who may find that

concentrating on people whose names begin with *L* or foods that begin with *E* takes his mind off the impending visit to the dentist, the monster in the closet, the scary creaking tree branch outside, or whatever other concerns might keep him awake.

And, of course, when he drifts off to sleep, you're a winner too.

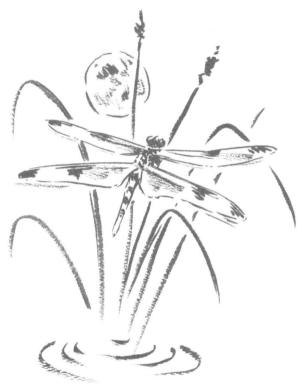

How Fortunate!

To play Fortunately, you start off with an unfortunate situation. Example: "I locked myself out of the house this morning."

Your child replies with a Fortunately, such as: "Fortunately, I had a spare key hidden under the doormat."

Now you need to contribute an Unfortunately: "Unfortunately, a bird carried the key off as soon as I lifted up the doormat."

Back to your child, who has to supply a Fortunately: "Fortunately, the bird's nest was in a tree right in my back yard."

Your turn: "Unfortunately, I didn't have a ladder."

Your child: "Fortunately, I was wearing spiked shoes and could climb the tree."

And so it goes, till no one can think of where to go from there, or until one of you has had enough, or until your child is asleep. In any of those cases, the game is over.

Fortunately.

ive Clues

Here's one more guessing game. In this case, the guesser is given exactly five clues, no more and no fewer, and either he solves the puzzle and wins or fails and loses . . . in one guess.

Give your child five clues to a secret object that you're thinking of, such as, "It's brown, it runs on electricity, it's in the living room, it's bigger than a shoebox, and it gets noisy sometimes." If he guesses (in one guess!) that it's the TV, he wins.

Or Would You Rather Have Tea?

Here's another game that doesn't usually get kids too worked up and so is suitable for quiet bedtime play: Coffeepot.

Do you coffeepot? Well, that depends on what "coffeepot" is . . . and guessing what it is is the challenge in this ages-old game. You think of a verb (if your child doesn't know what a verb is, say "an action word"). The verb should be a common action—brushing your teeth, eating, bathing, whistling, walking a dog, or some other reasonably ordinary occurrence. It doesn't have to be something you do every day. It doesn't have to be something *everyone* does. But it should be more common than piloting jet spacecraft or even yodeling, and something done more often than getting born or getting married.

Your child now has the traditional twenty questions in which to guess what the verb is. She substitutes the word *coffeepot* for the unknown verb as she asks the questions, which she hopes will help her figure out what the action is: "Do you coffeepot?" she might ask, or "Do I coffeepot?"

Other good questions are,

"Do you coffeepot indoors?"
"Do you coffeepot at a special time?"
"Do you coffeepot all year round?"
"Do you coffeepot in a special place?"

When she has guessed the verb, used up her twenty questions, or given up, it's her turn to think of a verb (action word) and your turn to guess what it is.

There is no penalty for wrong guesses ("Is 'coffeepot' 'dusting'?"), but each wrong guess does count as a question.

No Money Needed!

Another quiet game that will involve your child without getting her too worked up over winning and won't have her bouncing in bed with glee is I'm Going Shopping. This game requires that the child know her alphabet and be able to spell well enough to know what letter a word starts with.

In this game, the lead player says, "I'm going shopping and I'm buying ____." And she fills in the blank with something beginning with *A,* such as "apples."

The next player continues, repeating the *A* item and adding a *B* item: "I'm going shopping and I'm buying apples and bananas." The first player (or the third, if you're playing with two kids) might say, "I'm going shopping and I'm buying apples, bananas, and crayons." Note that it isn't necessary to list items that might really be found in a grocery store . . . or in any store. *C* could as easily be "chimpanzees." *D* could be "dogs" or "Dalmatians" or "daisies," as well as "doughnuts" or "dill pickles."

When a player can't remember the list, he's out of the game. The last remaining player wins . . . but of course, there's no reason you can't give your child hints and other help!

Most kids don't get too revved up or carried away in playing this game, which makes it a good game for tuck-in time.

Many Happy Returns and Exchanges

The Thirteenth Day of Christmas is another cumulative remembering game. In this case, the game assumes that you've gotten some pretty weird gifts for Christmas—even stranger than the leaping lords and maids a-milking of the famous song that inspired the game. And what do you do with gifts you don't want? You return them to the store, of course.

But, as with the original song (and with other cumulative remembering games), players are required to recite and remember an ever-longer list of items. The lead player (let's say it's you) starts off, "On the thirteenth day of Christmas, I returned to the store one ____" and names one of something unusual . . . perhaps one striped gnu.

The second player (and if you led off, it's now your child's turn) adds two of something to the original item, so she would say something like, "On the thirteenth day of Christmas, I returned to the store two purple trombones and one striped gnu." The third player—you again, unless you're putting two kids to bed at once—would add three of something to the two items on the list, and might come up with, "On the thirteenth day of Christmas, I returned to the store three pet skunks, two purple trombones, and a striped gnu."

If you can get up to twelve without messing up, you've both won; otherwise, the player who forgets an item, or re-members wrong, is out, and the other player is the winner. (In a three-player game, when one player is eliminated the other two continue to twelve or till one of the remaining players is eliminated.) As with I'm Going Shopping, there's no harm in giving your child help or hints.

Think, Thank, Thunk

This pastime doesn't involve winning/losing, doesn't count the number of guesses it takes to think of the object that's to be guessed at . . . it's just fun for the small set.

You say something like, "I'm thinking of the biggest thing in the living room," or "I'm thinking of something blue in my bedroom," or "I'm thinking of something wooden in the kitchen." Then she has to guess what the thing is you're thinking of. Depending on the child's age (and frustration tolerance), you can give broad clues and hints, minimal clues and hints, or give no help other than saying, "No, that's not it," or "Yes. You've got it."

Really little kids may need such guidance as, "No, the big flowerpot isn't blue; it's green." Very leading clues like, "Think what's in the kitchen drawer by the fridge," or "It's a piece of furniture. You sit on it," are certainly permissible.

After you've thought of something for him to guess at—or perhaps after a few times around, or on another night when you play this same game—let him think of the object to be guessed at while you do the guessing.

"I Know What You're Talking About"

Here's a pastime that's related to the previous one: Your child starts describing something, and you have to see how quickly you can guess what he's talking about. He should be encouraged not to give too-broad clues (such as "It keeps our food cold" or "She barks" or "It's where we wash our hands"), but he's not allowed to give misleading clues either.

For example, for a pencil he might say, "Most of them are yellow," "It's round, but the sides are flat," "The more you use it, the shorter it grows," "It starts out longer than your finger, but thinner," "One end is pink."

He should not say, "You write with it," or "It has an eraser on the end."

This game sharpens your child's powers of description.

Ell-tay E-may Ow-hay 🐷

One evening at bedtime, you can teach your child to speak Pig Latin, if he doesn't already know. Then, on occasional future evenings, you can have bedtime conversations in Pig Latin . . . just for fun.

In case you don't remember the rules of the "language," here's how to form words in Pig Latin:

Take the initial consonant sound (which may be one or more consonants, such as the "tr" of "trash," the "b" of "bell," the "sh" sound of "should," the "d" of "dog") and put it at the *end* of the word, followed by the sound "ay" (to rhyme with "way"). "My dog" becomes "Y-may og-day."

If the initial sound of the word is a vowel, you simply end the word with the syllable "way," so that "oh" becomes "oh-way," "and" becomes "and-way," and "I" becomes "I-way." The sentence "Oh, no . . . no way!" becomes "Oh-way oh-nay . . . oh-nay a-way."

Good Night . . . in Any Language

Give him a short lesson in a foreign language. Hold or touch his foot and tell him, *"El pie."* Get him to repeat it. Hold his hand and tell him, *"La mano."* Have him repeat that. Then hold his foot again and ask him, "What is this?" If he remembers the Spanish for foot and answers, *"El pie,"* praise him. If he doesn't remember *"El pie,"* repeat patiently without making him feel he has let you down or "failed." If he remembers *el pie* and *la mano,* try *el dedo* (the finger), or perhaps *la cabeza* (the head), or *la boca* (the mouth) or *el ojo* (the eye).

Of course, if you don't speak Spanish but do speak French, German, Finnish, or whatever, use whatever language you speak.

If he's mastered the major body parts in Spanish (or whatever language you're teaching him), you can proceed on another night to the days of the week or months of the year, rooms in a house or articles of clothing, or to the alphabet or counting in that language. Or teach him the parts of the body in a different language.

You can even teach him simple
sentences when he's mastered the
words you want him to learn.

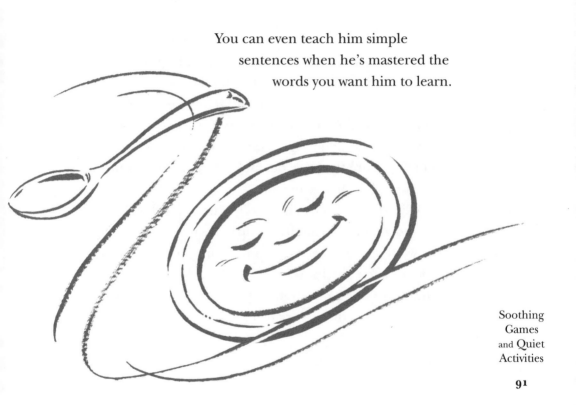

How Many Meeses?

English can be a fun language to play with, though it's certainly a confusing language for non-English-speakers (and kids!) to learn. Take plurals. The plural of *mouse* is *mice,* but the plural of *house* isn't *hice.* And the plural of *mess* is *messes,* but the plural of *hippopotamus* isn't *hippopotamuses*— it's *hippopotami.* Counting cats? One pussy, two pussies. Counting more than one octopus? They're not octopusses or octopussies; they're octopi.

Where is all this leading? To having fun with plurals. You and your child can dream up some just-for-fun plurals that would never be accepted in an English lesson but are good for a few giggles at home. And giggles are good for getting kids in a happy frame of mind, which is how you want them at bedtime (or anytime).

Rockin' the Night Away

If your childhood hasn't receded into the too-dim past, you probably remember how to play Rock, Scissors, Paper (known in some localities as Scissors, Paper, Stone). If not, your child may have learned already, in which case she can teach you. But just in case you don't remember and she hasn't yet learned, here are the basic rules:

Each player puts one hand behind her back (presumably her right hand, unless she's a leftie). There, unseen, she holds it ready in one of three configurations: held out flat ("paper"—the flat palm represents a flat piece of paper), in a fist ("rock"—the rounded fist represents a roundish rock), or with her ring and pinkie fingers curled up, and her index and middle fingers extended and spread ("scissors"—the two spread fingers represent the two blades of a scissors).

The two of you count in unison, "One-two-three," and on "three" you each bring your hidden hand into view so you can see what representation each of you has: rock, paper, or scissors. If you both have the same thing, the game is a tie. Otherwise, one or the other wins, according to the following list:

Rock and paper: Paper wins, because paper wraps rock.
Rock and scissors: Rock wins, because rock dulls scissors.
Scissors and paper: Scissors wins, because scissors cuts paper.

Of course, if your child is the hyper-excitable type, this game may not be a good choice of settle-down activity— she may become keyed up in her glee over winning (or frustration at losing). But for the average child, a few rounds of Rock, Paper, Scissors is quiet fun. And, because the game is so much a matter of chance, she has as good a chance of besting you as of losing. Now, what child doesn't feel good when she can boast, "I beat Mommy [or Daddy] at a game!"?

Altered States

Here's another short, fun game that's suitable for bedtime because it doesn't require any equipment and won't get your child worked up into an excited state.

Stand next to the bed and tell him to take a good look at you. Let him study you for as long as he wants to. Then go out of the room and change one thing about your appearance. You can unbutton a button (or button an unbuttoned top button or perhaps a pocket button), tuck in or untuck a shirt or blouse, remove a belt, untie a shoe or remove your shoes, put on or take off your glasses, or go to greater lengths by getting a tissue or handkerchief to put visibly into a pocket, applying lipstick if you have none on, doing something different with your hair, or even changing your pants, skirt, or shirt for a different one.

Now challenge your child to discern what the difference is. What have you changed? Will he be able to spot what you've done?

Soothing
Games
and Quiet
Activities

95

A Capital Idea!

Here's another challenge to occupy your child's mind (and make her feel smart when she knows many of the answers): As you tuck her in, ask her to name as many as she can of the state capitals. Sit by her side on the bed and praise all the ones she gets right. Give hints and help when she falters.

Since you've probably forgotten many of them yourself, here's a quick refresher course:

Alabama: Montgomery

Alaska: Juneau

Arizona: Phoenix

Arkansas: Little Rock

California: Sacramento

Colorado: Denver

Connecticut: Hartford

Delaware: Dover

Florida: Tallahassee

Georgia: Atlanta

Massachusetts: Boston

Hawaii: Honolulu

Idaho: Boise

Illinois: Springfield

Indiana: Indianapolis

Iowa: Des Moines

Kansas: Topeka

Kentucky: Frankfort

Louisiana: Baton Rouge

Maine: Augusta

Maryland: Annapolis

Michigan: Lansing

Minnesota: St. Paul

Mississippi: Jackson

Missouri: Jefferson City

Montana: Helena

Nebraska: Lincoln

Nevada: Carson City

New Hampshire: Concord

New Jersey: Trenton

New Mexico: Santa Fe

New York: Albany

North Carolina: Raleigh

North Dakota: Bismarck

Ohio: Columbus

Oklahoma: Oklahoma City

Oregon: Salem

Pennsylvania: Harrisburg

Rhode Island: Providence

South Carolina: Columbia

South Dakota: Pierre

Tennessee: Nashville

Texas: Austin

Utah: Salt Lake City

Vermont: Montpelier

Virginia: Richmond

Washington: Olympia

West Virginia: Charleston

Wisconsin: Madison

Wyoming: Cheyenne

Alpha-Best

For kids just learning their alphabet, who enjoy showing off their growing mastery of the skill, a simple recitation of the alphabet may be a good settle-down activity.

And for a child slightly more advanced, who's learning some words that start with each letter, running through the alphabet and naming a word that starts with each letter is a great way to show off knowledge, practice it a little more . . . and settle into bed for the night.

Older kids, who know their alphabets perfectly well, may enjoy making up nonsense words for each letter. (*A* is for "arfazoeey," *B* is for "bodimation," *C* is for "carna-mong," *D* is for "dittlypeeper," and so on.)

An Old-Fashioned Walk

The last suggestion for this category isn't technically a bed-time activity, it's a *pre*-bedtime activity. A mother of very young twins tells me she takes her kids by the hand and walks them around the entire house about an hour before bedtime. As they walk, they talk about whatever comes to mind, and they also look for things that are out of place.

The things they think of to talk about may be prompted by what they see as they walk (or not—it doesn't matter). The conversation makes for a good quiet "sharing time." The things they see that are out of place—mainly toys that need to be put away—are dealt with, neatening the house in the process and teaching the kids that toys should be put away at the end of the day.

And the walking helps use up the kids' energy and get them more ready for bed. They know, too, that after their "walk" comes story time, when they'll be getting into bed, and because they've grown accustomed to this sequence of events, there's minimal resistance to heading for bed after the walk.

Silly Rhymes, Fun Songs, and Loving Lullabies

There are certain things that are comforting and sooth-ing aurally. When the child hears them, she is lulled. Simple, quiet songs—not only the standard lullabies but other songs that fit this description—are one such thing. Spoken rhymes and rhythms are another. There is comfort in the familiar, but although the old stan-dards may carry the added benefit of familiarity, new rhymes and songs can soon become just as familiar, through repetition.

Any Soothing Song Can Be a Lullabye

Your five-year-old may feel she is too old for "Rock-a-Bye Baby," but that doesn't mean you can't sing her to sleep with a soothing song. Sing a soft, familiar nursery song, such as "London Bridge" or "Twinkle, Twinkle, Little Star" to your child. You can simply sing to her or suggest she sing along.

Other songs are suitable too, from old standard children's songs (perhaps you remember some from your own childhood) to folk songs (such as, "She'll Be Coming 'Round the Mountain" or "On Top of Old Smokey") to songs from *Sesame Street* or Disney movies.

Old Tune, Suitable New Words

Here's a new bedtime song you already know the tune to.
Sing the words to the tune of "Oh, Susannah," but at a
slower tempo.

> Oh, the sun has set,
> The day is gone,
> It's time to go to sleep.
> Oh, your sheets are cool,
> Your blanket's warm,
> Your pillow's nice and deep.
> Good night, sleep well
> Until the birdies peep.
> Oh, I'll see you in the morning
> But right now it's time to sleep.

Silly Songs,
Fun Rhymes,
and Loving
Lullabies

This Boat Sails for Dreamland

The child who is too big to be held and rocked can still be held against you and rocked . . . especially if you make a game out of it. And . . . what do you know?! I just happen to have a simple rhyme you can rock your child to.

Let him sit up in bed, while you sit next to him, holding him to you. As you hold him, rock him, and rhythmically recite (or read) the following poem:

> Rock-a-boat, rock,
> Down at the dock.
> Gentle waves hold
> You in their fold.
> Rock me, waves, please,
> Feeling the breeze.
> Down at the dock,
> Feel the boat rock.

If you like, just to be playful, on the line about the breeze you can purse your lips and blow a breeze across your child's face.

Lull-a-Boy, Lull-a-Girl

Kids love to make up songs. Their tunes will never win
Grammys, and their rhyme and meter is often off,
but they have fun doing it . . . so ask your
child to make up a lullabye
and sing it to you!

Rhyme Your Way to Bed

Here's another silly rhyme with accompanying actions that will ease your child into bed. At first, you can say it (or read it) to your child. After a few nights, when she's beginning to get it memorized, encourage her to say it along with you. Perhaps eventually she'll want to say it all by herself, without any help from you.

What the exact actions are that you pair up with some of the words is up to you. She can hold up her pinkie and thumb when she mentions them, or she can wiggle them. She can point to her eyes, blink them, or close them when she mentions her eyes. She probably wants to point to her ears when she mentions them. But as to the actions that deal with getting in bed, snuggling down, and so on, she should follow those words pretty closely.

Here is the rhyme:

This is my pinkie, and this is my thumb.
I'm getting in bed, and I'm counting to one.
These are my eyes. Are they brown? Are they blue?
I'm lying down snug, and I'm counting to two.

These are my feet, and I'm wiggling them free.
I'm stretching and settling and counting to three.
These are my ears. I have one, and one more.
I'm rubbing the sheet, and I'm counting to four.
These are my hands; under covers they dive.
I'm comfy in bed, and I'm counting to five.
I've counted to five, so now turn out the light.
My bed feels so cozy. I love you. Good night.

Silly Songs,
Fun Rhymes,
and Loving
Lullabies

Hooooooow Slllooooooooowly Cannnnnnn Youuuuuuuuuu Siiiiiiiing?

Instead of you singing to lull your child into a relaxed, sleep-inducing state, why not let him do it himself? Make a game of it—without telling him your true motive, of course! Suggest that he see how slowly he can sing an old favorite, such as "Twinkle, Twinkle Little Star," or "I've Been Working on the Railroad." Show him what you mean by singing the first few words yourself, in an exaggeratedly slow manner. Drag the syllables out, singing *verrrrrrry, verrrrrrrry slooooooowly,* then tell him it's his turn. Let his own slow singing slow down his body's pace, his own voice soothe him.

Rhyme Time

Play a very simple rhyme game with your child. Say a word and ask him for as many rhymes as he can think of for that word. If you say, "star," will he think of *car? Far, are, jar?* If you say, "me," will he think of *he, three, whee, we, see, tree, see, she, key* . . . ?

You can even let him give you a word for you to make rhymes for, since kids love turning the tables on their parents.

For a more advanced rhyme game, make up a simple line that ends with a word that has a common sound. (Hint: Try for a one-syllable rhyme—that is, "bright" rather than "brightly," or "home" or "dog" rather than "nearly" or "reason," unless you're playing with an older child.) Now ask your child if she can come up with a rhyming line.

For example, you say, "The moon is shining on that tree." Your child might add, "I like the way it shines for me."

Don't try to write a whole long poem. One line to rhyme with the first one is enough.

Silly Songs,
Fun Rhymes,
and Loving
Lullabies

109

New Rhymes for Old

Another rhyme game involves finding new lines for old poems. If you say, "Twinkle, twinkle, little star," your child should now come up with a new rhyming line that replaces, "How I wonder what you are." She might say, "You look as if you're very far." Or "I'd like to drive there in our car."

You can pick lines from nursery rhymes or other poems she knows or songs she's familiar with. Try "Little Bo-Peep has lost her sheep" (will she rhyme, "But maybe they'll come home to sleep"?) or "Jack and Jill went up the hill" (will she rhyme, "They reached the top and just stood still"?). Just try to pick short lines that end in simple sounds that rhyme easily.

See Lee? Silly!

Here is another silly rhyme for a small child that can be a stand-in for a story on a hurried night or a "bonus" treat after a story:

> Nighty-night, turn out the light.
> It's time for bed. Lay down your head.
> Here come two arms that will hug you real tight.
> Here is your mom who will kiss you good night.

(If it's his dad who's tucking him in, of course you'll substitute "dad" for "mom" in the last line.)

A Silly Rhyme for Night-Night Time

Here is a silly rhyme with accompanying hand motions. You can say it to your child as he lies in bed, before you kiss him good night. This is good for a small child, either on a night when there's no time for a story or even as an extra treat after his story.

First the poem itself:

Fingers and toes, here it goes.
One two three, on his knee.
On the bed, on his head.
Makes his belly shake like jelly.
In his hair, everywhere.

Now, here's what motions go with the rhyme (or you can make up your own): On the first line, touch his fingers and then his toes as you mention each. On the second line, tap his knee lightly three times with a finger. On the third line, tap the bed once and his head (forehead or top of head) once. On the fourth line, put your hand down flat on his tummy and wiggle it back and forth lightly. And on the last line, run your fingers through his hair on the word *hair* and then trail your fingertips down his side to his toes (through the blanket is fine, if he's all tucked in).

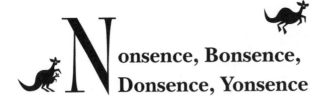

Nonsence, Bonsence, Donsence, Yonsence

Here's one more silly rhyme, a nonsense rhyme this time, to lull little ones with:

Eenie meenie inka-boo.
Crunka runka, bedtime for you.
Onka wonka bliddly bleep.
Minka, pinka, go to sleep.

Good Night . . . All of You

Now here's a soothing refrain that doesn't rhyme but coaxes your child into a relaxed state and suggests sleepiness to her. I've used "Wendy" for the child's name, but you'll put your own child's name in instead . . . unless, of course, your child is named Wendy! As you mention each body part, rub that part gently.

> Wendy's feet are going to sleep.
> Wendy's legs are going to sleep.
> Wendy's hands are going to sleep.
> Wendy's arms are going to sleep.
> Wendy's body is going to sleep.
> Wendy's eyes are going to sleep.
> Wendy is going to sleep.
> Good night.

Silly Songs,
Fun Rhymes,
and Loving
Lullabies

Starring . . . Your Child!

Here's another rhyme in which you'll insert your child's name. There are a few finger motions involved, too.

I've written the rhyme using a two-syllable name, "Danny," but if your child is named Seth (one syllable), Jonathan (three syllables, emphasis on the first), or Diana (three syllables, emphasis on the second), the rhyme still works . . . and I'll show you how. I'll explain the finger motions, too. Ready?

> High up on the mountain,
> Low down by the sea,
> Lived a boy [girl] named Danny,
> Happy as can be.
>
> Through the day's excitement
> Our boy [girl] loves to roam.
> But when it is bedtime
> Danny comes back home.

Danny is in bed now.
Close your eyes real tight.
Sail on dreams till morning.
I love you. Good night.

Now, here are the finger motions:

As you say, "High up on the mountains," touch the child's nose with your fingertip. When you say, "Low down by the sea," touch his toes through the covers. On "Our boy [girl] loves to roam," finger-walk up his arm. On "Danny comes back home," finger-walk back down his arm till you briefly squeeze his hand. When you say, "Close your eyes real tight," put a hand over his eyes. And as you say, "Sail on dreams till morning," "sail" the flat of your hand down from his eyes, across his chest, to his belly. Naturally, after "I love you. Good night," you'll kiss him.

Additionally, if you wish, you can use a funny, high voice for comic effect on "High up on the mountains," and a deep, rumbly voice for "Low down by the sea," continuing the rest of the rhyme in a normal voice.

Now, what if your child's name isn't two syllables?

Instead of "Lived a boy named Danny": For a one-syllable name say, "Lived a boy they call Seth," or for three syllables with the stress on the second syllable, "Lived a girl, Diana." With a three-syllable name with first-syllable stress (for example, "Jonathan"), you can squeeze in the extra syllable into the rhyme as it is shown.

Instead of "Danny comes back home": "Our Seth comes back home," "Jonathan comes home," or for three-syllable names with second-syllable stress, squeeze it in, "Diana comes back home."

Instead of "Danny is in bed now": Say, "Jonathan's in bed now." For three syllables with second-syllable stress, squeeze it in: "Diana is in bed now." And for one-syllable names, "Our Seth is in bed now."

What Time Is It?

This simple, lulling song, which tells your child it's time to sleep, is sung to the tune of "Twinkle, Twinkle, Little Star" (which, of course, is also the tune used for the Alphabet Song):

> Soon the moon at you will peep.
> Now it's time to go to sleep.
> Stars will shine way overhead,
> Making sure you're safe in bed.
> Down a mountain very steep.
> Meet me in the land of sleep.

Soft and Gentle Thinking

Another way to relax a child is to get him to think about pleasant things. They may be as mundane as his favorite candy, or as out-of-the-ordinary as fabulous animals that have never been seen on this (or probably any other) planet.

The conversations you have with him quietly, one on one, when you aren't hassling about chores or homework or cleaning his room, when it's just the two of you having a quiet, enjoyable talk, may be some of his favorite memories when he thinks back to these years later on.

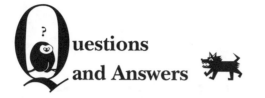

Questions and Answers

Ask him questions about his day: "What was the most fun you had today?" Concentrate on the positive, rather than "What would you change about today if you could?"

You can also, of course, ask him, "What's the best thing that ever happened to you?" or "What's your favorite memory?" The catch here is that these questions may invoke memories so exciting that he gets all charged up again. It's safer, for that reason, to concentrate on mundane, day-to-day happenings. If his favorite memory of the day is when the kindergarten teacher called on him and he knew the answer, or when his best friend gave him the baseball card he needed to complete a set, he'll get a nice, warm glow remembering, but he's not likely to get all revved up again the way he might if he remembers some major, exciting event.

Other questions designed to give him a gentle glow, rather than induce serious excitement in him, include

🦋 What's the prettiest thing you've ever seen?

🦋 What's the prettiest place you can imagine?

🦋 What's your favorite kind of dog?

🦋 If you could have
any animal at all for a pet,
what would it be?

Soft and
Gentle
Thinking

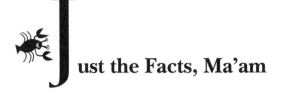

Just the Facts, Ma'am

You can challenge your child to find one new fact, or a list of five (or any other number) new facts, once a week or on certain evenings, and present them to you at bedtime.

For little ones, not yet of reading age, the "fact" can be that the tree outside his window is starting to show buds or to turn brown, or that the moon is full again, or that the moon can be seen in the daytime when it's located far enough away from the sun!

Kids of reading age can be encouraged to look up their facts in any book or Web site they please—an encyclopedia, almanac, school textbook, library-borrowed biography, or otherwise—though facts gleaned through observation should in no way be discouraged.

Praise your child for every fact she looks up and reports back, every observation she makes, every new bit of knowledge she gleans. Whether she is learning to do research or simply learning to be an aware person who walks around with her eyes open, noticing things, she's forming good habits either way.

And, of course, you can turn the tables by offering to bring an equal number of new facts to this bedside discussion yourself. If your son or daughter learns about Betsy Ross or why trees change color in the fall, why baby teeth fall out or how cartoons are made, it may not feel like "education" to him, and yet he'll still be learning something as he settles in for the night.

Now tell me what's wrong with that!

A Future as a Scriptwriter?

Ask your child to imagine a conversation between two fictional characters and tell you what they said to each other. They don't have to be from the same book or story. It's fine if he has Winnie the Pooh talking to Cinderella or Aladdin involved in a conversation with Red Riding Hood.

This is similar to some of the storytelling activities mentioned in Part 1, but here you're not asking him to write a whole story. You just want to know what Rapunzel might have said to the Big Bad Wolf, or what Hans Brinker and Eloise might say to each other.

You can suggest a topic of conversation, or a place where they might meet, to sharpen his focus a little: "If Winnie the Pooh came to the Prince's ball and danced one dance with Cinderella, what do you think they might have talked about while they danced?" "If Hans Brinker met Eloise while he was skating on the ice, what do you think they would have said to each other?"

These Are a Few of Her Favorite Things

Another way of putting your child in a good frame of mind, which will help her relax and get to sleep, is to ask her what her ten favorite things in the world are. As she lists them, she'll focus on them, not on closet monsters, or the way her teacher criticized her today, or other concerns.

Note: Don't ask this question when it's very close to her birthday, Christmas, or some special event like a trip to the circus. Your question may elicit a reference to one of these events as a response, and then she'll start thinking about her birthday party, or the clowns, or what Santa's bringing. With the event so imminent, she's likely to become excited and not relaxed at all. Save this technique for when there's no Big Occasion right around the corner.

i, Grandma!"

Ask him, if he were writing a letter to Grandma or talking to her on the phone right now, what he would tell her. (If the conversation veers off into unpleasant waters and he starts "telling Grandma" about the fight he had with a friend or the math test he's worried about, gently switch to another activity.)

"Hi, Grandma!"— For Real

In fact, your child actually can talk to Grandma as he settles down for the night in bed . . . without having to have a bedside phone extension and without incurring the cost of a long distance call if you live halfway across the country from Grandma.

All you need is a cassette recorder.

Your child can talk into the recorder while you operate it (or operate it himself, if he's older) and "tell Grandma" (or Aunt Jill or Cousin Kyle) all about his day—and, unlike the activity above, in this case Grandma will actually get to hear what he's telling her.

You can save up a week's worth of recordings, then send the tape off to Grandma, or you can make the tapings a once-in-a-while occurrence and send the tape off immediately.

(They'll give Grandma a better idea of some questions to ask him the next time she calls him, too.)

Out on a Limb of the Family Tree

Does your child get confused by who's who in your family? If he's really young, he may not understand that Uncle Ralph is actually your brother, or that Uncle Ted is Dad's sister's husband.

For little kids, a simple explanation is in order—and likely will need repeating from time to time. For older kids, a simple drawing showing the family tree, with Grandma and Grandpa connected on one side, Pop-Pop and Gram on the other, their respective (grown) children, those children's spouses, and, in turn, their own children may make things a little clearer to your child.

If she sees it on paper, she may finally grasp that Cousin Brittany is Dad's sister's daughter, or that Uncle George is actually Grandpa's brother.

Not only is this an engrossing bedtime activity, it will give her a better grasp of family connectedness that will stand her in good stead at the next extended family get-together.

Nothing but the Best

Here's another soothing exercise for your child's mind. Ask her what's the best thing about being . . . well, a lot of different people . . . and things. For instance, what does she think the best thing is about being a mommy? Or a daddy? What does she think is the best thing about being a dog? Or a cat?

Here are some others she can think of:

A doctor   A snail
A butcher   A bunny
A businessperson   A dinosaur
A construction worker   A dragon
A teacher   A kid
A sailor

The Magic Bed

"This is a magic bed. It can take you anywhere you want to go. The only fuel it needs is your imagination. Okay, now . . . where do you want to go tonight?"

So begins an imagined adventure for your child, to be engaged in as he lies beneath the covers. He may imagine his bed taking him to the moon, to DisneyWorld, to the Old West, or to Grandma's house. He may imagine a visit with the Three Little Pigs or Robin Hood or King Arthur, or he may be in a forest, hunting dragons, capturing unicorns, or even wrestling a bear.

The only caveat is that if he gets so involved that he starts getting excited, you may need to call a halt. After all, these activities are aimed at settling him down, not revving him up. But most kids, most of the time, will remain cozily quiet under the covers while their imaginations wander.

If he doesn't have a particular destination in mind, you can pick one out. Some suggestions include:

- Various foreign countries (especially ones he has some knowledge of, for example Holland, if he's old enough to have read *Hans Brinker*, or any country that you have relatives living in or that he's studied about in school)

- Alaska (unless you live there in reality)

- Hawaii (unless you live there in reality)

- Sherwood Forest

- Santa's workshop

- The top of Jack's Beanstalk

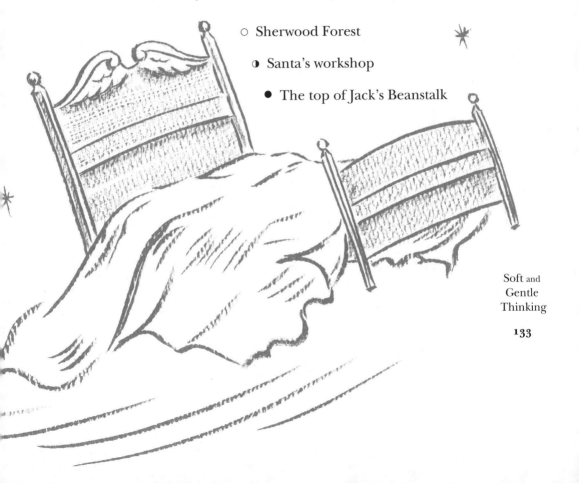

○ The Old West

Ask him questions about what he's doing and what he's seeing on this magical trip he's taking.

○ Whom does he see nearby?

○ What are they doing?

● What does the place look like?

○ What is the weather like?

○ How are the people dressed?

○ Are there any animals nearby?

● Are there trees or flowers? What kind?

"May I Borrow Your Antlers?"

You might call this thinking exercise "Crazy Mixed-Up Zoo." Think about the following questions: Would a mouse look like a moose if he had antlers? Could a rabbit make a habit of wearing snakeskin on his paws? What would happen if a cow laid eggs or a chicken gave milk?

Give your kid (and yourself) a little giggle or two by imagining one animal borrowing a trait from another animal. How many such silly combinations can your child think of? *Bonus thinking activity:* Name the resultant "new" animal in each case. For example, what would you call a mouse with antlers? Would a milk-giving chicken be a chickenow? Or a cowicken? *Second bonus thinking activity:* What sound would each of these new, combination animals make? Would a mouse with antlers still squeak . . . or bellow like a moose . . . or make some new sound altogether?

Soft and
Gentle
Thinking

135

Creature Features

Ask him to invent a fantastic creature—a made-up animal—and describe it. How big is it? What sound does it make? What does it eat? Where does it live? Is it friendly or ferocious? How would he go about catching one?

Holidazed

I think we all agree that holidays are fun. Wouldn't it be fun to add some more to the calendar? Suppose your child could declare a holiday . . . or two. What sort of holiday would he invent?

Ask him to dream up one or more new holidays. Here are some things to think about:

☺ The reason for the holiday. What (or whom) does it celebrate?

☾ The way the holiday is celebrated. What would be done on that holiday to make it a special day, a different day? Would it be marked by picnics, large family get-togethers, solemn observance, playing games, honoring a special person, or what?

⊕ The foods that would be traditional for this holiday. Birthday cakes go with birthdays, and turkey goes with Thanksgiving—is there any particular food that would be appropriate for your child's invented holiday?

🌙 Special decorations. Christmas brings trees and wreaths. Jack o' lanterns are in many houses when it gets close to Halloween. And some families go all out with acorns, pine cones, gourds, or colorful leaves to decorate the house around Thanksgiving. Would this holiday involve any special decorations, and if so, what are they?

🐭 Any other details. Is there anything else that would be connected with this holiday, any special way of dressing, any special games to play, any particular customs that would be appropriate for this special day?

Silly Willy

To someone who doesn't know what's going on, someone who doesn't have the basic information, even the most commonplace actions can be interpreted strangely. Kids sometimes misinterpret what they see because they lack some basic information.

Silly Willy *always* gets it wrong.

For instance, Silly Willy saw a boy eating cereal and wondered why the boy was putting the stuff in the bowl in prison inside his mouth. Silly Willy saw a girl walking a dog down the street and wondered where the dog was taking the girl to.

How many "Silly Willies" can your child think of?

A *Reeeeeeaaaaaallllly* Big Bed

Here's a good starting point for an interesting, informative discussion with your child that's suitable for bedtime: If all the kids in the world went to bed at the same time . . . in the same bed . . . how large a bed would you need? The idea is mind-boggling—not to mention silly, of course. It's also improbable. Why? Here's where this train of thought is going:

Not all the people in the world go to bed at the same time. And I'm not just talking about 8:00 bedtime as opposed to 10:00 bedtime.

This one, for older kids, requires an understanding of time zones, or at least of the idea that the sun shines on different parts of the world at different times. The concept is informative; it should hold your child's attention, yet it's not likely to rev him up.

If your child is old enough to grasp the concept of time zones, or the fact that the sun shines on only half the world at a time, you can point out that when kids in New York, Boston, Miami, or other Eastern Time-zone cities and towns who go to bed at 9:00 are snuggling under the sheets, kids in Chicago, Austin, and other Central Time-zone cities and towns are still an hour away from bedtime. Kids in the Mountain Time zone are probably just having dinner (assuming they eat around 6:00), and kids in L.A. and other Pacific Time-zone locations are playing or doing homework . . . because it's only 5:00 there!

Now . . . what about kids in Australia? What does your child think they're doing? (Clue to you: When it's 8:00 P.M. Eastern Time, it is respectively 9:00, 10:00, and 11:00 A.M. in the three different time zones of Australia.) In what other countries might kids be getting up, going to school, or at some other point radically different in their day than bedtime?

Stretch Those Imagination Muscles!

Ask other imagination-stretching questions. Here are some examples:

- ☏ If space visitors landed in our yard, what would you show them?

- ℂ If you could grow candy in your garden, what would you grow?

- ⊕ If someone from another country came to visit you, what do you think he'd like to see?

- 𝔇 If you had four hands instead of two, what could you do that you can't do now? What if you had four feet instead of two? Suppose you had suction cups on your hands and feet? What else would you like to have?

- ☏ Suppose you had a tail? What would you do with it?

- ℂ If you had eyes in the back of your head, what could you do that would be special or different?

⊕ What super-powers would you like to have? What would you do if you found you were invisible? What if you could walk through walls? What if you had x-ray vision? What if you had super hearing? What if you could fly? What if you could jump as high as the tallest building? What if you could make yourself grow or shrink any time you wanted to?

☽ If you could wish for any one thing, what would it be?

☽ Suppose a genie offered you three wishes, but you couldn't wish for anything for yourself—what would you wish for?

☾ If you could live anywhere, where would you choose to live, and why? If you could live anywhere at all—not just on Earth—would you choose to live somewhere else?

⊕ If you could be anyone else, who would you choose to be? Why?

☽ If you could trade places with someone for just one day, who would you want to trade places with?

☽ If you could be any TV character or cartoon character, who would you want to be?

☾ If you could meet any famous person from history, who would it be? What would you like to ask him or her?

☉ If you could have any real person, of any age, as a sister or brother, who would you pick (and why)?

☽ If you could have any fictional person, of any age, as a sister or brother, who would you pick (and why)?

☿ Lots of dogs are named "Spot," "King," "Rover," and "Fido." Think of some more inventive, imaginative names for dogs. Now how about cats?

☾ Dream up a recipe for an unusual sandwich.

☉ If you were an athlete, what sport would you like to play? Why?

☽ If you were a cow, what would you do you don't do now?

☿ If you were a horse, what would you do you can't do now?

Night-Night

144

☾ Suppose you were a bumblebee—what would you do?

☉ If you were a snake, what would you do that you don't do as a kid?

🌙 If you were a frog, what would you do that you don't do now?

🪐 Suppose you were a monkey—what would you do differently from your present life?

🌑 If you were a cat, what would you do differently from your life now? (Add or substitute other animals in accordance with the child's own interests—from dinosaur to dragon to unicorn to guinea pig or hamster.)

🌕 What do you think a horse might like to do that a pigeon does?

🌙 Do you think cows ever wish that they were chickens? Why?

🪐 Do you think chickens ever wish that they were cows? Why?

🌑 Do you think a monkey ever wishes he were a bird? Or vice versa? Why?

Think of good explanations for some of the things we see around us. I'm not looking for the right answer. I want creative answers, fun answers. For instance:

🌙 What makes the moon grow and shrink?

Ⓨ Why do the leaves fall off the trees in autumn?

Ⓒ Why does the sun rise?

◍ Why do beavers build dams?

ⅅ Why are some clouds white and some dark?

Ⓨ Why does the wind blow?

Ⓒ Why is your shadow sometimes taller, sometimes shorter?

◍ Why do rivers flow instead of standing still like the water in a swimming pool or a bathtub?

ⅅ Why do stars twinkle?

Ⓨ We didn't always know about all the planets being out there. Suppose more planets are discovered in the future. What do you think they might be called?

Ⓒ What would make your school a better school?

◍ If you could have any job in the world when you grow up, what would it be?

ⅅ Suppose it were a job that doesn't even exist now. . . . Invent a job that may not exist, but that you'd like to have when you grow up.

🐾 If you could be any animal in the world, what animal would you like to be? Why? What are the good things about being that animal? Is there anything about being that animal that isn't good?

🎄 If a Christmas tree could think, what do you suppose it would think?

🐟 What do you suppose a fish thinks?

📺 You know the way a remote control makes a TV work, right? Suppose you could control other things with a remote control? What would you like to have a remote control for? What would it do?

🚲 Pretend you're riding your bike, and suddenly it takes off up into the sky! Where do you go? What do you see? Where does it land? Does anything interesting happen to you when it lands?

🏖 Suppose you're at the beach and you're digging in the sand. Suddenly you find a treasure chest. What would you do?

🔥 Suppose every time you opened the door of your microwave oven, you found hot food in it? What would you do with all that food?

➊ Pretend you are an unhappy prince or princess. You have a castle, servants, and lots of money, but you're not happy. Why? What would you need in order to be happy?

➋ Suppose you were ten feet tall for just one day? What would you do?

➌ What if Practical Pig's house didn't have a fireplace for the wolf to fall into?

➍ What if someone else's foot had been small enough to fit in Cinderella's slipper, and the Prince got to that other woman's house first?

➎ What if Wendy, Michael, and John had chosen to stay in Never-Never Land with Peter instead of flying home again?

➏ What if the crocodile's clock hadn't run down, and it wasn't able to sneak up on Captain Hook

➐ If you could invite any person, real or fictional, to have dinner with us, who would you invite?

➑ What would you do if you found a secret door in the basement?

What would you do if you discovered a secret formula for making things invisible?

What would you do if a tree in your backyard suddenly grew way up into the sky?

About the Author

Cynthia MacGregor, with nearly forty published books to her credit, loves writing and says, "There isn't anyone in the world I'd want to trade lives with." Most of her books are either for kids or for parents, though she does write on other subjects as well. "I don't want to be a one-trick pony," she says. Her hobbies are writing haiku and cooking. Her web site is *www.CynthiaMacGregor.com.*